Eugene J. Hall

Poems of the Farm and Fireside

Eugene J. Hall

**Poems of the Farm and Fireside**

ISBN/EAN: 9783337256647

Printed in Europe, USA, Canada, Australia, Japan

Cover: Foto ©Thomas Meinert / pixelio.de

More available books at **www.hansebooks.com**

# POEMS

OF THE

# FARM AND FIRESIDE.

'TIS CHRISTMAS EVE, BUT THE STOCKIN'S DON'T HANG BY THE CHIMBLEY THERE.—*Page 59.*

# POEMS

OF THE

# Farm and Fireside.

BY

EUGENE J. HALL,

AUTHOR OF STORIES OF A WINTER NIGHT; CALEB COMERFORD,
FOOTPRINTS IN THE SNOW; WON AT LAST,
MANKIND IN GENERAL, ETC.

CHICAGO:
JANSEN, McCLURG & COMPANY.
1875.

Entered according to act of Congress, in the year 1874, by
JANSEN, McCLURG & COMPANY,
In the office of the Librarian of Congress, at Washington.

Electrotyped by A. Zeese & Co.

TO

MARY, MY WIFE,

MY

KINDEST CRITIC

AND

TRUEST EARTHLY FRIEND.

# PREFACE.

The following poems are neither the result of hours of idleness nor the imperfect fancies of one who has had nothing else to do. Most of them have been written in the editorial room, with the worry of printers and the hurry of newspaper work about the writer. He has received many words of encouragement from his friends, and has been gratified by the kindly reception some of them have met with from the press and the people.

All have been written with a purpose; some to point out the abuses that are common in society, to show their deplorable effects and the means of reform; some to create a kindly feeling towards the poor and lowly; some to exhibit a few peculiar phases of human nature, that have come to the author's observation; some to describe the joys, the sorrows and the experiences of the human heart, and every one with the earnest intention and sincere hope of doing good.

As literary achievements, the author does not claim any high degree of excellence for them, nor does he expect the approbation or the applause of literary persons. They have been written for the people; and to the working people, among whom the author has passed the greater portion of his life, he looks for encouragement and patronage. If therefore they meet with a friendly welcome from those for whose good they are intended, he will feel that his efforts in their behalf have not been in vain.

E. J. H.

# CONTENTS.

## POEMS OF THE FARM AND FIRESIDE.

| | |
|---|---:|
| Old Farmer Brown, | 17 |
| The Women's War, | 25 |
| Hard Times, | 32 |
| Christmas Eve, | 39 |
| Away Down East, | 43 |
| Rufus Rawlin's Ride, | 47 |
| Old Holden, | 50 |
| Theresa Trott's Dream, | 52 |
| Contentment, | 54 |
| A Morning in July, | 58 |
| September, | 60 |
| October, | 62 |
| Leila and Jane, | 63 |
| "Help Me Across," | 66 |
| After the Summer Time, | 68 |
| A Home Picture, | 69 |
| The Old Clock in the Corner, | 70 |

## MISCELLANEOUS POEMS.

| | |
|---|---:|
| Marah, | 77 |
| Twilight, | 83 |
| Tabitha Topp, | 87 |
| Victoria Grey, | 91 |

## Contents.

| | |
|---|---|
| World Weary, | 95 |
| Midnight, | 97 |
| Helen, | 99 |
| Twice Asleep, | 100 |
| Then and Now, | 101 |
| Solomon Ray, | 103 |
| Two Pictures, | 105 |
| On the Bank of the Murmuring Rill, | 108 |
| True Friends, | 111 |
| Sleep, | 112 |
| Another Year, | 113 |

# ILLUSTRATIONS.

| | |
|---|---:|
| FRONTISPIECE—'Tis Christmas Eve, but the stockin's don't hang by the chimbley there, | 4 |
| Hannah, I'm sick a livin' here, an' a workin' from spring to fall, | 19 |
| And, kneeling down on the time-worn floor, both bowed their heads in prayer, | 23 |
| An' liftin' my hands up to heaven, I prayed for a speedy reform, | 27 |
| Josiah Johnson started and went his homeward way, | 33 |
| Bread an' butter are gittin' high an' wages are gittin' low, | 37 |
| She turns from the window and lingers awhile by the open door, | 55 |
| The leafless trees are brown and bare, | 71 |
| And beneath the waving branches oft we told our tales of love, | 80 |
| Miss Tabitha Topp, a young lady in town. | 86 |
| That she thought herself charming was plain to be seen, | 91 |
| She wearily sighs—"And women must weep, And the sooner it's over the sooner to sleep, | 94 |
| A child, of beauty rare, with a cherub face and golden hair, | 105 |
| A loathsome wretch, in the dungeon low, With the face of a fiend and a look of woe, | 107 |
| On the bank of the murmuring rill, | 109 |

(13)

# POEMS

OF THE

# FARM AND FIRESIDE.

# POEMS

## OF THE

# FARM AND FIRESIDE.

### OLD FARMER BROWN.

#### INSCRIBED TO THE PATRONS OF HUSBANDRY.

From the harvest field old Farmer Brown came home with a look
    of care,
He threw his hat on the floor, and sat down on his old splint-
    bottomed chair.
He wiped the sweat from his dripping brow, and pulled out his old
    jack-knife,
He whittled away to himself, awhile, and called to his little wife.
From her quaint and tidy kitchen, she came through the open door;
With her sleeves pinned up to her shoulders and her skirt pinned
    up before.
She looked as faded, wrinkled and worn as the folds of her gingham
    gown,
When she saw the haggard and hopeless look on the face of Farmer
    Brown.
Then, down on her rocking-chair she sank, in a sort of helpless way,
Nor spoke one word, but listened and looked to hear what he
    might say.

"Hannah, I'm sick a livin' here, an' a workin' from spring to fall
A raisin' 'taters an' corn to sell, that don't bring nothin' at all.
Here we have worked together, for forty years, like a pair o' slaves.
An' that old *mortgage* ain't lifted yet, that I owe to Gideon Graves.
That judgment note o' Deacon Dunn's, will soon be fallin' due.
An' where the money's a comin' from, why, I can't tell, nor you.
I'm kept in sech a worry an' fret, by all o' these sort o' things,
That I have to sell the stuff that I raise, rite off for what it brings.
It costs so much for my taxes now, an' to keep the wolf away,
That I haven't no chance to make a cent, an' that is what's to pay.
Hannah, we've both on us grown old, an' our children all are gone,
There is no one now that is left at home for us to depend upon.
I ain't as strong as I used to be, nor as able to work, I know,
But I've got to set these matters square, an' the farm 'll have to go.

"Half o' the world lives idle, with plenty to eat an' wear,
An' the ones who work the hardest, have often the least to spare.
The farmers work till their forms are bent, an' their hands are hard an' brown;
The workmen delve in the dust an' smoke, o' the workshops in the town;
The sturdy sailors bring to our shores the wealth o' foreign lands,
An' the other half o' the world subsists, by the work o' these hardened hands.
An' this is one o' the reasons why, I can't pay what I owe;
While you an' I are a gettin' old, an' the farm 'll have to go.

"I've worked in the woods in the winter time, I've plowed an' sowed in the spring,
I've hoed an' dug through summer an' fall, an' I haven't made a thing.
Sometimes I lie awake all night, an' worry an' fuss an' fret,
An' never a single wink o' sleep, nor a bit o' rest I get.
I think of our grown-up children, an' the life they've jest begun —
They've got to hoe the same hard row, as you an' I have done.
I think o' the politicians, an' the way they rob an' steal,

HANNAH, I'M SICK A LIVIN' HERE, AN' A WORKIN' FROM SPRING TO FALL.

An' the more I think o' farmin', the poorer it makes me feel.
The speculators buy up our cheese, our butter, our wool an' hay;
An' they sell 'em ag'in for more'n twice as much as they had
    to pay.
They bleed us in transportation, they fleece us everywhere;
They cheat us on our provisions, an' the very clothes we wear.
They live in their lofty houses, on the best that can be found,
Their wives wear dazzlin' diamonds, an' their children loaf around.
In the summer they go to the sea-shore, an' the springs, to make a
    show,
An' that is the way our butter an' cheese an' our corn an' 'taters go.

"We work in the sun all summer, raise turnips an' corn on shares,
That the railroads an' politicians may cheat us an' put on airs.
They carry the reins o' power, an' will till we fill our graves.
They rule an' ruin the markets, an' we are a pack o' slaves.
What's to be done? God only knows. I've failed in many ways,
In tryin' to lay a leetle by, to ease my declinin' days.
I never have been a shiftless man,—I've figgered, I've worked an'
    tried,
While the old farm's been a runnin' down, since the day that father
    died.
I've borrowed money to pay my debts, an' I've watched the interest
    grow,
Till it's fairly got the start o' me, an' the farm 'll have to go."

Then the little wife of Farmer Brown stood up upon the floor,
And she looked at him in a kind of way that she never had before,
The furrows fled from her shriveled cheeks, and her face grew all
    aglow:
"*I never* will sign the deed, John, an' the farm shall *never* go.
There's jest one thing to be done, as sure as you an' I were born,
You must join the GRANGE an' *vote*, John, if you would sell your
    corn;
Hope an' prayer are good, John, for the man who digs an' delves,
But Heaven will never help us, John, unless we help ourselves.

I ain't as chipper an' smart an' spry, nor as strong as I used to be,
But I've got *a heap o' spunk*, John, when it's started up in me."

Over the old man's furrowed face, the tears began to flow,
He never had felt more proud and strong, since their wedding long
    ago.
A golden gleam of heavenly hope, illumined his soul's despair,
And, kneeling down on the time-worn floor, both bowed their heads
    in prayer.

AND, KNEELING DOWN ON THE TIME-WORN FLOOR, BOTH BOWED THEIR HEADS IN PRAYER.

## THE WOMEN'S WAR.

### A LAY OF THE LAST CRUSADE.

Well, Amos, I've been to the meetin', we held it at Barker's to-
    night;
I tell you the Lord is a comin' in all o' his power an' might.
The glad songs o' Zion are ringin', in places not used to the sound,
Where our boys have been wastin' their evenin's, in drinkin' an'
    loafin' around.
All over the land that we live in, in country an' town, everywhere.
We're a goin' to give Mr. Tyndall a test o' the power o' prayer.

I've been to the meetin' at Barkers', we give him a sudden surprise;
When he looked up an' seen us a comin', I tell you he opened his
    eyes.
He stared at us over the counter, each eye looked as big as the
    moon,
But we wan't to be frightened in that way, we walked right into
    the saloon.
He didn't attempt to oppose us, he was willin' to give us fair play;
He looked all around him an' chuckled, but never a word did he say.
There were lots o' young men there a loafin', I reckon a dozen or
    more;
When some on 'em seen us a comin', they slid out the leetle back
    door.
Some stood by the counter a drinkin'; they hadn't an atom o'
    shame,
An' those who were playin' at billiards went on with their impious
    game.
The rest on 'em sot there a sippin' their whisky, their brandy an'
    gin,

A lookin', a leerin', a winkin', an' waitin' for us to begin.
I gazed at the bright lookin' bottles behind the tall counter displayed ;
I thought o' the lives they had wasted ; I thought o' the graves they had made.
I thought o' the boys they had ruined, by leadin' 'em widely astray ;
O' the wrongs they had wrought on the helpless, by stealin' their substance away ;
An' all o' the power within me, swept over my soul like a storm.
An' liftin' my hands up to heaven, I prayed for a speedy reform.
While, out o' the mouths o' the sisters, who solemnly knelt by me there,
A hundred impressive responses j'ined in with my passionate prayer.
Then we sung that glad hymn o' salvation, "O turn ye, for why will ye die ?"
An' it seemed to my soul in that moment, God's glory was comin' so nigh.
We sang o' the lowly Redeemer, an' those that he perished to save.
An' when the last stanza was ended, the room was as still as the grave.

Bill Barker looked over his counter, the prospect he didn't enjoy ;
'Twas plain to be seen he was thinkin' o' those he had helped to destroy.
He glanced at the row o' bright bottles before his broad mirror arrayed,
Like one who is proud o' his power, nor cares for the wrecks he has made.
But soon o'er his hard-lookin' features a kinder an' softer look stole ;
Perhaps some good angel was tryin' to soften his sin-burdened soul.
He looked sort o' troubled an' worried, an' still he had nothin' to say ;
He seemed to be quietly wishin' we women were out o' the way.
All was still ! till a wild-lookin' woman, with a face jest as white as a shroud ;
Crept stealthily out o' a corner, an' stood in the midst o' the crowd.
Her holler cheeks spoke o' starvation, her sunken eyes told o' distress ;

AN' LIFTIN' MY HANDS UP TO HEAVEN, I PRAYED FOR A SPEEDY REFORM.

Her quiverin' lips o' mute anguish no language o' mine can express,
She lifted her talon-like fingers high over her head in despair,
An' walkin' straight up to the counter, she gazed at the rumseller there.
He looked at her pale, haggard features, an' turned with a shudder away.
He spoke not a word, but he listened to hear what the woman would say.

"Look! Look on your work here, Bill Barker," she cried with a passionate wail;
"You have ruined my home an' my husband, and sent both my young boys to jail.
They say I am *mad!* do you wonder? Your liquor has brought all my woe;
I tell you your time is a comin' — *God's judgment is certain but slow!*"

Then turnin' away from the counter, she silently passed from the place;
The rumseller's conscience was troubled, he showed it all over his face.
His mind seemed to be all unsettled, his feelin's he couldn't control;
I knew that a powerful struggle was goin' on down in his soul.
An', Amos, I reckon, no language can picter' the way that he felt:
He looked kind o' sorry an' 'umble, like one jest beginnin' to melt.
An' when in a few moments after, we j'ined in a season o' prayer,
He silently came round the counter an' noiselessly knelt by us there.
The men had all finished their playin' an' drinkin', and stood by the wall,
An' over their rough-lookin' faces the tears were beginnin' to fall.
The sounds o' the revel were over, the air seemed more pure and serene;
An' all on us felt in that moment, the presence o' angels unseen.

As soon as we finished our prayin', Bill Barker rose up from the floor,
An' while we stood wonderin' an' gazin', he started an' opened the door.
Then, takin' a barrel o' liquor, he rolled it along with his feet;
He knocked out its head with a hatchet an' spilt it out into the street.
Then all on us turned in an' helped him to finish what he had begun :
He emptied his bright-lookin' bottles, nor paused till the good work was done.
Then turnin', he said, "I'm a goin' to close up my business to-night :
I've made up my mind to be honest, I mean to try hard and do right.
I've sent more young men to destruction than any man livin' in town,
But I'm goin' to put up my shutters, an' tear my old liquor sign down.
I'm goin' to work, an' God willin', I'll be a respectable man ;
Go on with the good work you're doin', I'll help you as much as I can."

Then when he was through with his speakin', we all commenced singin' again,
An' "Nearer my God to Thee, nearer to Thee," was our joyful refrain.
An' those who had been there a drinkin', seemed moved by the power o' prayer,
An' sang with the deepest o' feelin' the words o' that heavenly air.
An', Amos, I can't help believin' that music went up to the sky,
To be chanted an' echoed in Heaven, by beautiful angels on high.

Yes, Amos, I've been to the meetin', you needn't look smilin' nor queer,
That we are goin' to conquer, I haven't a doubt nor a fear.

You may laugh an' may say that we women are crazy an' out o' our
    heads;
That we'd better be darnin' our stockin's, a sweepin' or makin' the
    beds;
But we're goin' right into the battle, nor will we give up in despair;
If we only go at it in *earnest*, there's a wonderful power in prayer.

## HARD TIMES.

From the noise of the busy workshop, at the close of a winter day,
Josiah Johnson started, and went his homeward way ;
His face was black and dusty, his hands were cold and bare,
And through the holes in his garments, he felt the frosty air.
Weary and worn, he grumbled, at the hardness of his lot ;
He came at last to his dwelling, a low and cheerless cot.
The broken panes of the windows were filled with wads of straw,
The kitchen was damp and smoky, the old stove would not draw.
His wife was pale and sickly, she never had been stout,
He found her hardly able to labor or be about ;
He looked at her haggard features, he gazed at her faded gown,
He hung his hat on a rusty nail and, with a sigh sat down.
Then, looking up at his wife, he said, in a melancholy way :
"What is the use I'd like to know, o' workin' from day to day?
Nothin' comes o' my labor, but a pittance mean an' poor,
Hardly enough to keep the wolf away from our humble door.
I don't believe there's a man in town that works more hours than me,
An' yet I'm ragged an' pinched an' poor, an' wretched as I can be.
I never have been lazy, I never have loafed around,
A steadier man than I have been, 'aint nowhere to be found :
But I never seem to prosper, however hard I try,
An' there's nothin' left for me to do, but to dig along, an' die.

"I don't know what is a comin', I wouldn't think it strange
If our country should go to ruin, unless there comes a change.
It is loaded down with public debts, an' I am much afraid
That none o' our children's children will live to see 'em paid.
Our cities an' towns are bonded for more than they can bear,
An' the people are pinched an' worried with taxes everywhere ;
From the coast o' Californy to the piney woods o' Maine,

JOSIAH JOHNSON STARTED, AND WENT HIS HOMEWARD WAY.

## Hard Times.

Our debts grow like a torrent in the time of a heavy rain.
"Where has the money gone to? It isn't hard to tell!
Go into our city councils an' look a leetle spell;
Go visit our legislatures wherever they may be,
An' lookin' *under the surface* jest see what you can see;
Regard the pitiful picter an' turn in shame away,
Nor wonder that our loved country is a goin' to decay.

"The standard o' public honor, is gittin' mighty low,
While truth an' patriotism are things o' the long ago.
Our laws are made by loafers, to sudden greatness grown,
Whose intimate acquaintance I'd be ashamed to own;
Who load the people with burdens they cannot well endure.
Who vote themselves the moneys, exacted from the poor.

"A man who runs for office, is covered with mud an' slime,
By half o' the worthless idlers an' loafers o' his time;
He must spend his money freely, an' give the lion's share
O' the spoils o' his public office to the half who send him there.
He must visit the vilest places, an' listen to curses loud,
And pay for plenty o' liquor to treat a drunken crowd;
He must stand at the pollin' places when election day comes 'long,
An' beg an' buy an' dicker for the votes of a vulgar throng.
An' all o' the money he squanders in bribin' these greedy knaves,
He steals ag'in from the people when he gits the place he craves.
No man o' truth an' honor will stoop to things so low,
If ever he runs for office he don't have any show.
So fellers are sent to congress, to vote themselves more pay,
An' the times keep gittin' harder an' harder every day.
Hard times! hard times! is the common cry in every place I go,
Bread an' butter are gittin' high an' wages are gittin' low;
Our business men are a breakin' up, our banks are goin' to smash,
An' everybody is deep in debt an' greatly in need o' cash.
A hard, cold winter is comin' on with all of its want an' woe,
God pity the poor an' the hungry ones, with nowhere on earth
  to go."

Then, after thinking a minute, Josiah Johnson's wife
Put down her pan of potatoes and laid aside her knife,
And standing up by the table, she said in a cheerful way,
" The times are a growin' better an' better every day:
It's only the worthless bottom that's fallen out o' things,
That's got up this commotion among financial rings.
'Tis goin' to be a blessin', it'll stop those frauds an' crimes,
An' reckless speculations that have helped to make hard times:
An' the day is swiftly comin', when things that are bought an' sold,
Will be paid for in hard money, in silver an' in gold.
An' as to the politicians that have plundered the land so long,
You may be right in some things an' in most may not be wrong.
The only way for to reach 'em an' humble their guilty souls,
Is to go with your feller workers an' face 'em at the polls.
Stand up for men o' honor on every election day,
An' tend to your daily duties an' labor an' hope an' pray.
Remember when you are weary, that hard times come no more,
When the troubles o' life are over, an' we walk on the golden shore."

BREAD AN' BUTTER ARE GITTIN' HIGH AN' WAGES ARE GITTIN' LOW

## CHRISTMAS EVE

In an old New-England kitchen, where a warm and cheery fire
  burned,
Sat good old Farmer Ketcham, and his wife, one winter night.
The wind without was wailing, with a wild and woeful sound,
And the feathery flakes of the drifting snow lay deep upon the ground;
But what cared Farmer Ketcham, for the tumult out-of-doors?
For he had sheltered the cattle, and done the other chores,
And snug in the chimney corner, in his easy-chair, he sat,
Silently smoking his old clay pipe, and petting the purring cat;
While, plying her knitting needles, his wife rocked to and fro,
Humming a hymn and dreaming a dream of the long ago.
Over the old-time fire-place, a rusty musket hung,
And a score of strings of apples from the smoky ceiling swung,
While back in a dingy corner, the tall clock ticked away,
And looked like the sagging farm-house, that talking to decay.
The knitting fell from the woman's hands; the old man turned also
He took his pipe from his mouth, and he slowly knocked the ash
  out,
And after thinking a moment, he said, with a solemn air,
" 'Tis Christmas Eve, but the stockin's don't hang by the chimbly
  there."

The woman sighed, and then replied, in a sad and shivering tone
"The years have come, an' the years have gone, an' we are all
  alone,
An' I have jest been thinkin' of a Christmas long ago,
When the winders were frosted over, an' the ground was white
  with snow;
When we sat in the chimbley corner, by the firelight's cheery
  gleam;

When our lives were full o' promise, an' the future but a dream;
When all o' the rest of our folks had gone away to bed,
An' we sot an' looked an' I listened to the whispered words you said.
Till home from Benson's store, came rollickin' brother John,
An' a peekin' thro' the winder, saw what was a goin' on.
Then how the neighbors tattled an' talked all over town,
Till you an' I were married, an' quietly settled down.

" While a rummagin' through the cobwebs, in the garret, t'other day,
I found a pile o' broken toys, in a corner stowed away,
An' a lot o' leetle worn-out boots, a layin' in a heap,
As they used to lay on the kitchen floor, when the boys had gone to sleep.
I looked at the worn-out trundle-bed, an' the cradle long laid by,
An' leanin' ag'in the chimbley there, I couldn't help but cry.
For the faces o' my children came back to me once more,
An' I almost heerd the patter o' their feet upon the floor.
I thought o' their happy voices, an' the leetle prayers they said,
As they used to gather 'round me, when 'twas time to go to bed.

" Of all the earthly treasures we prize in the world below,
The ones we love the fondest are the first to fade an' go,
Of all the beautiful children that came to our fireside,
The one we loved most dearly was our leetle girl that died.
Her eyes were blue, an' soft as the hue o' the cloudless summer air,
An' bright as a gleam o' golden light were her curls o' shinin' hair.
Her thoughtful face was white as the flakes o' the newly-fallen snow;
Too much of a leetle saint she was to live in the world below.
How calm in her leetle coffin she looked in her last repose,
As sweet as the fairest lily, as pure as a tuberose.
An' I can well remember the sadness o' the day,
When my heart was well-nigh broken as they carried her away.

" The eldest of our children was a proud an' han'some boy;
He was his father's brightest hope, an' his mother's pride an' joy.

I used to play with his chubby hands, an' kiss his leetle feet,
An' wonder if ever a babe was born more beautiful an' sweet.
An' many a night, by candle-light, when he was snug in bed,
I've patched his leetle clothes with weary hands an' an aching
    head.
We sent him away to college — he did uncommonly well,
Till he went to live in the city, an' married a city belle.
Of all our earthly trials, of all our earthly care,
The cold neglect of a thankless child is the hardest of all to bear.
His wife is a woman with only high notions in her head,
She couldn't knit a stockin', nor bake a loaf o' bread.
She plays on the pianner, nor works with her lily hands,
An' she talks in a foreign lingo that no one understands.

"The youngest of our livin' boys I never could understand;
He didn't take to larnin', no more 'n a fish to land.
He was wayward an' hard to govern, not altogether bad;
He was strong an' proud, an' set in his ways, but not a vicious lad.
An' somehow, we couldn't keep him quite under our control,
But I know he had a tender heart, an' a good an' noble soul;
An' a mother's prayers will go with him, wherever he may be; —
God keep him safe, an' bring him home, in his good time, to me.

"I miss our children's voices, for all have gone away;
One has gone to the better land, an' the rest have gone astray.
I wonder if up in heaven, where all is bright an' fair,
If we will meet our children, an' they will love us there."

There was a rap at the outside door, the old folks gave a start;
The woman sprang from her rocking-chair, with a flutter at her
    heart.
The door swung widely open, and banged against the wall,
And into the farm-house kitchen strode a stranger dark and tall.
The woman looked at his bearded face a moment in surprise;
She saw a quiver about his mouth, and a glad look in his eyes,
And lifting up her hands to Heaven, she uttered a cry of joy.

And bowed her white head lovingly on the breast of her wayward
  boy.

The red flames roared upon the hearth, the beech logs cracked and
  steamed;
And on the floor and time-worn walls, the firelight glowed and
  gleamed.
That old New-England kitchen had never been more bright,
Than it was to Farmer Ketcham and his wife that winter night.

## AWAY DOWN EAST.

Away down east whare mountain rills
    Ar' thru the hollers flowin';
Whare cattle browse upon the hills,
    When summer winds ar' blowin';

Whare in the moonlight winter nights
    The world puts on sich splendor,
When young folks go tu singin' school
    An' git so kind o' tender;

Whare village gossips hear an' tell
    The'r kind o' harmless slander;
Thare lived blue-eyed Mehetabel,
    An' honest young Philander.

Mehetabel was jest as sweet
    An' fair as summer weather,
She hed the cutest leetle feet
    That ever trod in leather.

An' then those mild soft eyes o' her'n
    Wy! cider wer'n't no clearer;
They made Philander's visage burn,
    Whenever he sot near her.

Philander, he was tall an' thin,
    A kind o' slender feller;
He hed a sort o' goslin' chin,
    His hair was long an' yeller.

Drest in his go-tu-meetin' clothes,
　　A standin' collar sportin';
He went down cross-lots Sunday nights,
　　To Deacon Spencer's courtin'.

Thare down he sot afore the fire,
　　A thinkin' an' a lookin';
He praised the deacon's sheep an' cows,
　　He praised *her* mother's cookin'.

He talked all round the tender pint
　　But somehow, couldn't du it,
His words got *kind o' out o' jint,*
　　Afore he could git thru it.

'Twas twelve o'clock one Sunday night;
　　A blazin' fire was roarin';
The old folks hed gone off tu bed;
　　The Deacon he was snorin'.

Around the time-worn room the light
　　Fell kind o' soft an' rosy,
The old pine settle it was drawn
　　Up by the fireplace, cozy.

Mehetabel sot on one end,
　　Philander he sot by her,
An' with the old tongs in his hand,
　　Kept pokin' at the fire.

He tried tu tell her how he felt;
　　It sot him in a flutter,
The sweat, it jest rolled down his face
　　Like drops o' melted butter.

So thare they sot an' talked about
　　The moonshine an' the weather,
An' kept a kind o' hitchin' up
　　Until they hitched together.

The Deacon snored away in bed;
    Philander he got bolder;
He slid his arm around *her* head
    An' laid it on his shoulder.

An' when she lifted up her eyes,
    An' looked up intu his'n,
It seemed as if Philander's heart,
    Intu his mouth hed ris'n.

He sot an' trembled for awhile,
    She looked so mighty clever,
Some spirit whispered in his ear—
    "*Jest du it now or never.*"

Sez he—"My dear Mehetabel,
    My house an' home ar' waitin',
An' ain't it gittin' tu be time
    That you an' I were matin'?"

An' then, sez she, jest loud enuff
    For him tu understand her,—
"If you kin be content with me,
    I guess it is, Philander."

The Deacon woke up from his dreams,
    Sez he: "Ther's suthin' brewin'."
He peeked out thru the bed-room door,
    Tu see what they were doin'.

An' when he saw 'em sittin' thare,
    Like leetle lambs in clover,
He almost snickered right out loud,
    It tickled him all over.

He nudged his wife and told her tu,
    An' my! how it did please her.
An' then they talked themselves to sleep,
    An' snored away like Ceazer.

Philander sot there all night long,
    He didn't think o' goin';
Till when the day began tu dawn,
    He heerd the roosters crowin'.

An' when he started over home,
    Alone acrost the holler,
He kept a talkin' tu himself,
    An' fumblin' with his collar.

Sez he: "Ther' never was a chap,
    That did the bizness slicker"—
An' then, he gin' himself a slap,
    An' my! how he did snicker.

An' now blue-eyed Mehetabel
    Is married tu Philander,
An' village gossips idly tell
    That ne'er was weddin' grander.

Those peaceful moonlight winter nights
    Have not yit lost the'r splendor,
The young folks go tu singin' school,
    An' still git kind o' tender.

AWAY DOWN EAST, whare mountain rills,
    Ar' thru the hollers flowin';
Whare cattle browse upon the hills,
    When summer winds ar' blowin'.

## RUFUS RAWLIN'S RIDE.

Thru Goshen Holler, whare hemlocks grow,
Whare the ripplin' rills with a rush an' flow
    Ar' over the rude rocks fallin';
Whare fox an' bear an' catamount hide
In the'r holes an' caves in the mountain side,
A circuit preacher once used to ride,
    An' his name was Rufus Rawlin.

He was set in his ways, an' what was strange,
If you argued with him he wouldn't change;
    You couldn't git nothin' thru him.
Solemn an' slow in style was he;
Slender an' slim as a tamarack tree,
An' allus ready tu disagree
    With everybody that knew him.

One night, he saddled his sorrel mare,
An' started over tu Ripton, whare
    He'd promis'd tu du some preachin'.
Away he cantered over the hill,
Past the school-house at Capen's Mill;
The moon was down, an' the evenin' still,
    Save the sound of a night-hawk screechin'.

At last he cum tu a dark ravine —
A feelin' kind o' queer, an' a mean
    Sensation stealin' o'er him.
Old Sorrel began tu travel slow,
Then gin a snort an' refused tu go;
The parson clucked, an' he hollered "Whoa!"
    An' wondered what was afore him.

Then, all of a sudden, he seemed tu hear
A gurglin' groan, so very near
   That it scattered his senses, nearly ;
"Go 'ome! Go 'ome!"— it loudly cried ;
"*Go 'ome!*" re-echoed the mountain side ;
"Go 'ome," away in the distance died,
   An' he wished he was home, sincerely.

An' then, afore his terrified sight,
A light gleamed out in the starless night,
   That seemed tu beat all creation.
Then thru the bushes a figger stole,
With eyes o' fire an' lips o' coal,
That tingled the parson's righteous soul,
   An' filled him with consternation.

He lost his sermon an' dropped his book ;
His hair riz up, an' his saddle shook
   Like a saw-mill under motion.
Never a single word he said.
But, suddenly turnin' old Sorrel's head,
Away an' out o' the woods he sped,
   An' put for the land o' Goshen.

Intu the streets o' Goshen town
The terrified parson cum ridin' down,
   In a fearful sort of a flutter ;
Swift as a strong September gale,
With his cloak a streamin' like Sorrel's tail,
With his eyes wide open, an' features pale
   An' whiter than winter butter.

He told the neighbors that he had seen
A fiend o' fire in Huff's Ravine,
   That had driven him back tu Goshen.
He told of its deep an' dreadful groans,

Of its doleful cries an' dismal moans,
Of its flamin' eyes an' rattlin' bones;
   An' it got up a great commotion.

An' stranger, it is many a day
Since Rufus Rawlin was laid away
   In the grave-yard over yander;
I was a boy in those glad hours,
As full o' my fun as the spring with showers:
'Twas me an' a son o' Jacob Powers,
   That got up all that wonder.

We took a punkin o' common size,
An' cuttin' some holes for the mouth an' eyes,
   We gin it the right expression:
Then hollered it out till its shell was thin,
An' puttin' a taller dip within,
It looked as ugly an' mean as sin —
   'Twould a scared a hull procession.

The night was dark as ever was seen,
An' nothin' was heerd in Huff's Ravine
   But the sound o' the water flowin';
The parson come, in a quiet way,
A smokin' his old brown pipe o' clay,
A thinkin' o' what he was goin' tu say
   When he got to whare he was goin'.

An' the fiend he saw, an' the rattlin' bones,
Were a punkin', a gourd, an' some gravel stones,
   That gin him all o' that glory.
Yet, never ag'in up the mountain side,
In the night, would Rufus Rawlin ride;
An' many a time I've laughed till I cried,
   Tu hear him tell the story.

## OLD HOLDEN.

Wal, John, they du say that old Holden is dead;
    An' he died without leavin' a will,
He was hit by a stick on the top o' his head,
    While rollin' a log in his mill.

An' now his relations 'll quarrel about
    His gold an' unsettled estate;
They 'll soon be a fightin' an' lawin' it out,
    As sure an' as certain as fate.

Now many may say that old Holden was rich,
    But no one 'll ever repeat
That he ever has helped a poor man from the ditch,
    An' has set him ag'in on his feet.

No, he plundered an' pinched, an' he cheated the poor,
    An' he hated all churches an' creeds;
But he's gone tu a place whare I'm certain an' sure
    That he 'll git the reward o' his deeds.

For, John, he was hated wherever he went,
    Wy! he hadn't an atom o' soul —
His gold wasn't lent without twenty per cent.
    An' a mortgage tu cover the whole.

'Tis said that a beautiful angel above
    Writes down in his book with a pen,
All the good that is done, every labor o' love,
    An' the follies an' failin's o' men.

An' thare they will stay, without fadin' away,
    'Till the race of us all 'll be run,
An' we'll all on us know, at the last judgment day,
    All the good an' the bad we have done.

The good an' the pure 'll have nothin' tu fear,
    An' John, I would rather be poor
An' penniless here, if my record is clear,
    An' my hopes o' the future are sure.

Old Holden is dead without sayin' a prayer:
    His death it was suddenly sent;
Wy! he hadn't a minnit tu think or prepare,
    Not a chance to reflect an' repent.

An' now all the riches he had at command;
    His houses, his lands an' his gold,
Will not open the gates tu the beautiful land
    That I fear he'll never behold.

## THERESA TROTT'S DREAM.

Theresa Trott is forty-five,
Still unmarried and yet alive,
    And plain as the years can make her.
She long has waited, has hoped and prayed —
Nevertheless she is still a maid,
And now is fated to feel afraid
    That no man ever will take her.

Once, o'er her shoulders, white and fair,
Had fallen her tresses of dark-brown hair —
    The pride of her former lovers;
Its hue has faded, and now, instead,
Is many and many a silver thread
In the little tuft, on the back of her head,
    Her white cap cunningly covers.

With her slippered feet on the fender there,
And her elbows resting upon her chair,
    She gazes into the fire;
With fingers open, and wrists turned in,
Forming a prop for her toothless chin,
She thinks of pleasures that might have been,
    As she watches the *sparks* expire.

Fair are the faces that come and go,
In the rosy embers that gleam and glow,
    And memories, sweet and tender,
Flare in the flames, that leap and play,
Flicker and fade, as they die away,
Leaving nothing but ashes gray
    On the cold hearth by the fender.

## Theresa Trott's Dream.

And, gazing into the cheerful blaze,
Theresa thinks of her bygone days,
    And memories without number
Rise in her mind — then her eyelids close
And, soon beginning to nod and doze,
Her somnolent senses court repose,
    And she sinks into a slumber.

In a beautiful dream, again she sees
The slender figure of Solomon Pease,
    Her happy and thoughtful lover.
Home from the conference meeting they go;
The moonlight gleams on the crispy snow
And the stars look down, with a tender glow,
    That beam in the skies above her.

She sees a home, where the firelight falls
With a cheerful glow on the kitchen walls,
    And her very heart rejoices,
As her eyes behold, in a corner there,
A manly form in his easy-chair;
And she hears the sound of a noisy pair
    Of laughing children's voices.

Then all of her fleeting fancies seem
Fading away from her joyous dream,
    And her dreamland fabrics falling.
Solomon Pease is old and gray;
The hopes of her girlhood have passed away
And, think as she will, and dream as she may,
    The past is beyond recalling.

## CONTENTMENT.

The golden morning is breaking,
    And the warm sun's slanting beams
Creep over the earth awaking
    From its quiet rural dreams.
The farmer's wife by the window stands,
Holding her dish-cloth in her hands,
With her heart as light and as free from care
As the birds that sing in the morning air.

She looks, through the open window,
    On a quiet and lovely scene —
A beautiful rolling prairie,
    With its waving carpet of green;
The morning dew is sparkling bright
On the blades of grass in the mellow light;
The sunbeams fall through the leafy bowers
Of the door-yard blooming with fragrant flowers.

On the barn-yard fence, her husband
    Is seated upon a rail,
Whistling a tune and drumming
    With his knuckles on a pail;
He casts his eyes o'er the verdant plain,
And thinks of his growing grass and grain,
And he says, with pride, "I'm a man of wealth,
With my well-tilled farm and my perfect health."

She turns from the window and lingers
    Awhile by the open door;
Her dish-cloth slips from her fingers
    And falls on the white pine floor;

SHE TURNS FROM THE WINDOW AND LINGERS AWHILE BY THE OPEN DOOR.

## Contentment.

The swallows sail through the summer air,
Over the meadows fresh and fair;
The lively crickets are chirping shrill,
While she talks to herself, as a woman will.

" Though many may have their wishes
    For fashion, for wealth and style,
Yet here I can wash my dishes,
    And be happy all the while;
Though lowly in life my lot may be,
There's a charm in my rustic home for me —
'Tis a hallowed place: it is fondly dear;
With God and nature, I'm happy here."

## A MORNING IN JULY.

The sun gleams over the mountains,
    And through the hazy air
It lightens the sombre hill-sides,
    And meadows green and fair.
It gilds the light clouds drifting
    Adown the summer sky;
There's beauty in the dawning
    Of a morning in July.

The birds are joyfully singing
    Amid the leafy boughs,
While into the pastures the farm-boys
    Are driving the glossy cows;
The busy bees are humming,
    The larks sing in the sky;
'Tis a picture of wondrous beauty,
    A morning in July.

I stand and dream of a morning,
    A morning bright and fair;
When I was a merry farm-boy,
    Without an earthly care.
I gaze on the grand old picture
    Of woodland, field and sky;
But I am a boy no longer,
    This morning in July.

The hills are here, and the mountains,
    The rocks and leafy trees,
From over the waving meadows
    I feel the fragrant breeze;

But those whom I knew have vanished,
    And older grown am I;
I sigh as I think of the changes
    Of this morning in July.

Ah! the dreams of youth are fleeting
    As the fancies that fill the mind;
In the race of life we are running,
    They soon are left behind.
I turn away from the picture,
    And think, with a mournful sigh,
Of the forms and friends that have vanished
    Since that morning in July.

## SEPTEMBER.

The winds are blowing soft and low,
    The days are drifting by;
The sunshine gleams in golden beams,
    The clouds float through the sky,
And every form of earth and air
Around me seems serene and fair.

The summer's bright and fragrant flowers
    Have faded, one by one;
Its last bright day has gone away,
    Its dreamy hours are done.
Now Autumn comes with crimson dyes —
The world in dying beauty lies.

Our lives go drifting on, and on,
    While summers come and wane;
The weal and woe of long ago
    Will never come again,
While new hopes rise on fancy's wing,
With every glad return of spring.

O may our summers, as they go,
    Be always bright as day,
And may no clouds like sable shrouds
    Drift o'er our peaceful way;
May fancy ever build her towers
In gardens blooming with bright flowers.

## September.

When earth and air no more are fair,
    When seasons come no more,
How sweet to feel the endless weal
    Of Heaven's celestial shore!
Where golden skies will ever rise
Before our eyes in Paradise.

## OCTOBER.

Gloomy clouds are flying past,
    And the cool October breeze,
Sighing with a mournful sound
    Through the branches of the trees,
Scatters Autumn's golden leaves
    Roughly o'er the world so drear.
Summer flowers have ceased to bloom,
    And the winter storms are near.

Homeward have the swallows flown
    To a more congenial clime;
And the song birds all are gone
    Like the fleeting summer-time.
Gathered is the golden grain
    From the stubble fields below;
Soon will nature lie at rest
    'Neath her wintry cloak of snow.

So the bright and tranquil hours
    Of life's spring and summer fail,
Bringing Autumn's golden hues,
    Bringing Winter's storm and gale.
Yet, when summer roses bloom
    In the fleeting world once more,
Man's divine, immortal soul,
    Wakens on a fairer shore.

## LEILA AND JANE.

### I.

The skies were bright and the world was fair,
The tall grass swayed in the mild June air;

The bees were humming amid the flowers,
And song birds gladdened the summer hours.

Two maidens wandered across the lea,
With hearts as happy as they could be;

They paused on a gently sloping hill,
And fell to thinking, as young girls will.

Sweet are the visions, and pure and good
Are the joyous fancies of maidenhood;

Those bright creations that come and go,
Painting the future with rosy glow —

As the sinking sun, with a parting ray,
Gilds the clouds of the dying day.

There came no shadow of grief or pain
To blue-eyed Leila or dark-eyed Jane;

Their happy hearts were as light and gay
As the brook that ran on its babbling way.

And Leila said: "In a future year
In wealth and splendor I will appear;

"And when, on a coming summer day,
My costly carriage may roll this way,

"The simple farmers, in great surprise,
  Will gaze in wonder, with dazzled eyes."

"And I," said Jane, "the wife would be
  Of one who marries for love and me;

"Give me a home, and a true love there,
  And for wealth and fashion I do not care."

The maidens paused, and both were still,
Then sighed together, as young girls will.

## II.

The summers pass and the winters wane
With blue-eyed Leila and dark-eyed Jane.

In a room where the dazzling gaslight falls
On velvet carpet and gilded walls,

On costly pictures and statues rare,
A woman sits in her easy-chair.

In the ruddy coals, that gleam and glow,
She sees the faces of long ago.

The picture dwells in her memory still
Of her summer-day dreams upon the hill.

Lines and wrinkles of grief and care
Have furrowed her features once so fair.

Ah, blue-eyed Leila! thy dreams were vain;
Thy life is saddened with grief and pain.

The happy hopes of thy youth have fled,
And life is nothing when love is dead.

There's a cheerful cottage that stands alone,
With woodbine and ivy overgrown;

## Leila and Jane.

The roses blossom about the door,
And the sunlight falls on the white pine floor;

The song bird's melody greets the ear,
And sounds of children, so sweet to hear.

And dark-eyed Jane by the window there,
With lines of silver amid her hair,

Looks o'er the meadow, towards the hill,
And thinks as only a woman will.

A house to shelter, enough to wear,
Enough for comfort and some to spare,

Little I asked of wealth or fame,
And all of my wished-for blessings came.

## "HELP ME ACROSS." *

The day was dying, the world was still,
The sun was sinking beyond the hill.

The clouds in the far west upward rolled,
In a gleaming flood of crimson gold.

Like a golden bar in the quiet skies,
Reaching from earth to paradise,

The last warm sunbeam slanting down,
Fell on a cottage old and brown;

And, through a window, gleamed and smiled
On the beautiful face of a dying child;

Peacefully fell, on her snowy bed,
Like a heavenly halo 'round her head.

Softly, she opened her dreamy eyes,
And gazing into the distant skies,

She saw a vision of perfect rest,
Beyond the light of the glowing west:

Saw white-winged angels, and afar
The golden gates of Heaven ajar;

And the form of her father, bright and fair,
In the crimson flood of glory there.

---

* "Sometime ago a little girl in Ithaca, just before she died, exclaimed—'Papa, take hold of my hand and help me across.' Her father had died two months before."

But a dark, deep river rolled between
The dreary world and that heavenly scene.

Yet, looking over the dismal tide,
She longed to stand by her father's side.

"Papa, take hold of my hand," she said,
"And help me across." The day was dead,

For the sunbeam paled and passed from sight,
And on that beautiful ray of light,

A soul ascended by angels borne,
To a world where mortals may never mourn;

Passed away from its earthly clay,
Like the glowing light of the dying day.

While a thousand beautiful angels smiled,
At the perfect faith of that holy child.

## AFTER THE SUMMER TIME.

Over the tops of the tasseled corn,
Over the harvest-fields forlorn,

Over the pastures, brown and bare,—
The balmy breath of the Autumn air,

In a tremulous tone, is borne along,
Like the plaintive waves of some sad sweet song.

The flowers fade, and the green leaves die,
And the months of the circling year go by.

Oh, life! like the months, we must pass away;
Like the falling leaves, we must soon decay.

From the flush of youth into manhood's prime,
We march in the endless course of time.

Then the faltering step and life's welcome close
The folded hands and the long repose.

## A HOME PICTURE.

A kitchen fire burns bright and red,
A little table is neatly spread.

In the lamplight sitting, alone and still,
A woman thinks as a young wife will —

"The world has many a weary care,
My life is simple and no less fair.

"Little of earthly fame have I;
Little of worldly wealth laid by;

"Yet a loving heart that is true and kind,
Is better than riches and fame combined.

"In my humble home will I remain,
Nor e'er of my lowly lot complain.

"Living and loving is sweeter far
Than all of the world's bright baubles are."

The cat wakes up on the kitchen floor,
The house dog barks outside the door.

Listening, the waiting wife can hear
The sound of a well-known footstep near.

The creaking gate is swung once more,
Her husband enters the open door.

And never a prince under palace dome
E'er met with a dearer welcome home.

## THE OLD CLOCK IN THE CORNER.

The leafless trees are brown and bare,
The snowflakes sweep through the frosty air.

With the wintry wind they sport and play,
As it wearily whistles the night away.

The time-worn clock in the corner stands,
With faded dial and rusty hands.

With ceaseless motion its pendulum swings,
And this is the doleful song it sings:

"Tick, tick, tick, there are smiles and tears
In the mournful tale of a hundred years.

"The voice of memory, soft and low,
Whispers to-night of the long ago.

"'There are friends you loved; there are hopes most dear,
That are dead and gone with the old, old year.'

"Spiders have woven their silken thread
In the dingy corner overhead;

"'Mid the endless dust of the busy day,
That hands now pulseless have swept away.

"The world will change, and time will fly,
And all grow old as the years go by.

"I have looked on a careless child at play,
And have heard his laughter loud and gay.

THE LEAFLESS TREES ARE BROWN AND BARE.

## The Old Clock in the Corner.

" I have seen a growing, bashful boy,
Full of the flush of health and joy.

" In raptures over a picture fair,
And a tiny curl of golden hair.

" I have seen him gaze, with manly pride,
On the fair sweet face of his new-made bride.

" I have heard an infant's plaintive cry,
And a careworn mother's weary sigh.

"And an aged father, old and gray,
Talking of years that had gone away.

" I have seen the sable pall and bier,
A lifeless form and the mourner's tear;

"And have heard those words, so often said,
Tenderly over the dear ones dead:

" 'Ashes to ashes, and dust to dust —
Life is fleeting and God is just.' "

O, memory! fond memory! thou phantom of our woe!
Thou sweet reminder of the dreams and hopes of long ago.

Thou living shadow of the soul, that ever comes at will,
When human lips have ceased to speak and human hearts are still.

# MISCELLANEOUS POEMS.

# MARAH.

> In the hereafter, angels may
> Roll the stone from the grave away.—*Whittier.*

Deep within my bosom buried, where no human eyes may see,
There's a world of tender memories, only known to God and me;
And my weary heart, o'erladen, seeks an outlet for its woe,
Like an earth-imprisoned fountain, long impeded in its flow.

Visions slowly rise before me, in intangible array,
Of a passion wild, eternal, of a love without decay;
Bright creations of my fancy, pictures of my dreaming soul,
Thoughts no human tongue can utter, or no human will control.

Gently raise me from the bosom of the world of common care,
And I seem a spirit, dwelling in bright castles in the air;
Misty forms about me gleaming, far above the halls of night,
Minarets of sparkling beauty, lifted into realms of light.

And I linger there, enchanted by the beauty of the place,
While an angel stands beside me, and she wears a woman's face:
Sleeping, waking, dreaming, thinking, wheresoever I may be,
Thoughts of her I cannot banish; she is all the world to me.

Pale and fair as sculptured marble seem her faultless features now,
Shining braids, in golden clusters, hang above her thoughtful brow;
Every nerve within my being trembles in her earnest gaze,
And the moments seem as lengthened into endless, happy days.

Drink the draught of joy, whose sweetness lifts the drooping spirit up,
And the dregs of MARAH linger in the bottom of the cup;

Bitter, always, to remind us, joy is ever mixed with tears,
And man's dreams of youthful beauty end in disappointed years.

Hope will come to man unbidden — it will mock him from afar,
Like the soul-enchanting beauty of a distant evening star;
Though his weary heart be burning with the fire of despair,
Hope will fan the flame till nothing is but dust and ashes there.

Hope, that fills man's soul with visions he would gladly drive away;
Hope, that builds anew the idols that he fain would have decay;
Charms him by her mystic beauty, holds him in her magic spell,
Leaving him to grasp at nothing, like a Tantalus in Hell.

Hope inconstant, hope delusive — ah! no idle words are these —
Brightest boon to mortals given, more infectious than disease;
Wherefore is the sense and reason, man should be to sorrow born?
Wherefore should his soul be blighted, and his heart be left forlorn?

Wherefore should his pride be humbled and his years be filled with pain?
Life unmixed with joy and pleasure is existence spent in vain.
Woman! woman! cold and distant, void of feeling, loving none;
Thou art but a soulless statue with a senseless heart of stone.

Thou would'st bury in the bosom of a dark and soundless sea,
One whose only earthly pleasure is the joy of loving thee.
In thy cold, imperious beauty, pride and wisdom are combined;
Thou hast God's great gift of GENIUS and a deep and thoughtful mind.

Thou hast friends to do thy bidding, and a fortune at command,
And a throng of ardent suitors boldly clamor for thy hand.
Votaries of wealth and fashion, gilded worshipers of style,
Seek, with amatory whispers, thy attention to beguile;

Seek to woo thee with their splendor, yet their proffers you decline;
What am I to hope for pity from a spirit proud as thine?
I have neither gold nor jewels, nor a mansion tall and grand,
I can bring thee simply nothing but an honest HEART and HAND.

AND BENEATH THE WAVING BRANCHES OFT' WE TOLD OUR TALES OF LOVE.

Fool am I to think such trifles could a soulless woman please,
Woman's proud heart opens only to the click of GOLDEN keys.
What to her are sense and reason, and a toiling hand and brain?
Nothing, nothing but a target for her cold and proud disdain.

For her love of admiration and her fondness for display
Seem to steal her better nature and her common sense away;
Seem to blind her nobler instincts with the filmy gauze of art,
Till she lives a soulless being, void of feeling and of heart.

Woman! woman! art thou happy as thou seemest to appear
'Mid the rustling throng of fashion, 'neath the blazing chandelier?
Resting on the silken cushions of thy carriage, rolling by,
Is thy proud and haughty spirit never troubled with a sigh?

All the shining gold of Ophir and a thousand gems beside,
Cannot calm the raging tempest of a woman's humbled pride.
Tho' she smiles in outward beauty, in the shining veil of dress,
There are sorrows in her bosom that no language can express.

When the summer skies were cloudless, oft we wandered in the grove,
And beneath the waving branches, oft we told our tales of love;
Curious eyes peered through the bushes, yet we heeded not their gaze,
Gaily sang the birds about us, those were happy halcyon days.

All the world I loved was with me in that beautiful retreat,
And my life seemed bright and lovely as the blossoms at our feet;
Yet those dreams we dreamed were fleeting, fleeting as the summer
    hours,
And the hopes we had have faded like the lovely summer flowers.

Wherefore should I idly murmur, wherefore should I sadly moan?
I will rid me of this sorrow, tho' it turn my heart to stone.
I will cast aside the gloomy and sad mantle that I wear,
And will drown my joyless passion in the world of common care.

Still the broad world lies before me, and afar my eyes can see
Grand creations proudly rising, shadows of the yet to be.

When thou art gone — Ah! come what may,
There are memories never to pass away,
When the stars come out in the quiet skies,
I shall dream again of thy tender eyes,
And gaze on thy features, pure and fair,
While I hear thy voice in the evening air;
And, smoothing the cares in my troubled breast,
These pleasant memories will bring me rest.

MISS TABITHA TOPP, A YOUNG LADY IN TOWN.

# TABITHA TOPP.

### I.

#### HER HOME AND HER LOVERS.

Miss Tabitha Topp, a young lady in town,
    Had a very great passion
    To lead in the fashion.
So she put on the airs to take everything down,
And she patronized art, in order to gain
    Perfection and grace,
    In form and in face,
In a manner I will not attempt to explain;
    But I only will say,
    In a much shorter way,
That she made up her BEAUTY by handsomely dressing,
Since nature had been rather spare with that blessing.

Of maids and dress-makers she had a full score,
And a carriage with monograms half covered o'er,
With a footman behind and a coachman before;
    Was it wonderful then,
    That all the young men
Should think her an "angel," an "exquisite creature,"
The very perfection of form and of feature?
She had broken the hearts of a dozen or more.

Her father was "wealthy," her lovers were "fine,"
As foppish and brainless as she could desire;
They swallowed her mother's bad grammar and wine,
And laughed at the wit (?) and stale jokes of her sire.

There had once been a time, in an earlier year,
When Topp was an humble retailer of beer,
Yet, by close calculation, by constantly saving,
By the fair smiles of fortune, by pinching and shaving,
He prospered at last in his worldly affairs,
And rose from the foot to the top of the stairs.

Of all the beaux with which "Tabbie" was blest
One suitor was sweeter than all of the rest.
His pink and white features, his exquisite airs,
His moustache of semi-invisible hairs,
His diamonds and rings, with his showy attire,
Were all that Miss Tabitha Topp could desire.
He was fond of fast horses, and fonder of drinking,
And fonder of billiards than working or thinking.
Whenever he called, Mrs. Topp took great pains
To give him a glass that "befuddled" his brains.

O, woman, fair siren, men cannot withstand
The cup of destruction that lurks in thy hand,
How oft have the noblest been led and beguiled
To taste the bright poison because you have smiled.
O, tempt not thy friend with the power that lies
In thy musical voice and thy clear, lustrous eyes.
Thy influence dazzles his brain like a mist,
Thy soft, pleading accents he cannot resist,
And yielding at last to thy subtle control,
He drinks and he dies, wrecked in body and soul.

## II.

### HER MARRIAGE AND WEDDING TOUR.

So Tabitha married Augustus Fitz Fooile,
And started away with her husband and poodle.
To Europe her lord kindly promised to take her,
So she was as happy as money could make her.

They crossed the Atlantic: they landed in France;
    They tarried at dissolute Paris awhile,
To patronize fashion and art, and to dance:
    There Tabitha carefully studied the style.
They visited Sicily, Venice and Rome.
Admired St. Peter's "magnificent dome."
Pronounced it a "temple of wondrous design,"
And its pictures of martyrs and saints "very fine."
They went to the Vatican — saw Pius IX.
They wandered together through elegant halls,
They gazed at the treasures of art on the walls,
The works of the masters, of which they had heard,
With their faded old faces, "looked very absurd."
They traversed the Alps, they descended the Rhine,
Viewed all the old ruins and notable places:
They thought "the old ruins, tho' striking and bold,
Would have looked very well if they wasn't so old."
They visited England — attended the races.
Then greatly "disgusted with foreign affairs,"
This new-married couple came home for repairs.

Now, if there was ever a silly extreme
    In popular folly, 'tis going abroad,
For half of our "European tourists" would seem
    Better fitted by nature to carry a hod.
"All must follow the fashion, as every one knows,"
So over the water each simpleton goes.

### III.

#### ADVERSITY.

Time glided away, with a great deal of CHANGE:
How many fond lovers a few years estrange.
Poor "Tabbie" grew older and thinner and whiter,
Forgot how to smile, and soon learned how to sputter,
Because her "Augustus would lie in the gutter":
In short, his attentions had ceased to delight her:

He drank and he gambled; he lived very fast;
Unregretted he died, with the tremens, at last.

Misfortune, 'tis said, never travels alone,
And "riches have wings," for they often have flown.
The house of the Topps, being largely involved
In wild speculations, the bubble dissolved;
There suddenly came a great financial crash
That carried away all their hopes and their cash.
The sheriff "came down like the wolf on the fold";
Their house and rich furniture had to be sold.
Now those who had loudly professed to admire
The Topps when they dressed in their showy attire,
Pronounced them exceedingly vulgar and plain.
The orthodox brethren all frowned with disdain,
And ceased to remember the Topps in their prayers
When they learned of the change in their worldly affairs.
Forsaken by friends (?) and avoided by all,
Even those they despised now rejoiced in their fall.

### MORAL.

There are sorrows and ruin, and want and distress,
And griefs that no language can speak or express,
That may come to a man with no will to abstain
From as trifling a thing as a glass of champagne.
And they on whom nature has deigned to bestow
A plentiful share of the good things below
Should not walk through the world too conceited and vain,
Regarding the lowly with haughty disdain.
They may fall from the top to the foot of the stairs
And crush all their proud, supercilious airs.

## VICTORIA GREY.

A GIDDY young girl was Victoria Grey,
One proud and determined to have her own way;
    And, rather than bend,
      She would lose her best friend,—
She was one upon whom one could never depend.

That she thought herself *charming* was plain to be seen,
By her confident manners and satisfied mien;
    She was one of that kind
      That one often will find
With a small, selfish heart and diminutive mind.

Victoria Grey had a passion for dress,
Tho' taste and good breeding she did not possess;
    On the street she would flirt,
      And sweep through the dirt,
With thirty-six yards of light silk in her skirt.

She had many lovers, it may be a score,—
She had promised to marry a dozen or more;
      All felt happy and gay
      At the confident way
They were flattered and loved by Victoria Grey.

Augustus Van Quirk was her fortunate flame
(Victoria loved his euphonious name),—
      A weak little fellow,
      Whose whiskers were yellow,
With little white hands and a mind rather mellow.

He took her to operas, dances and plays,
He won her affections in various ways;
      He whispered a store
      Of tender love lore,
That blighted the hopes of the dozen or more.

They were married at last; 'twas a famous affair,
Made brilliant by presents of real plated ware,—
      'Twas a transient display,
      The talk of a day;
And this was the end of Victoria Grey.

Five years have passed by, and Augustus Van Quirk
Has never been guilty of going to work;
      Just over the way
      Is a small sign to-day,
"BOARDING — Mrs. Van Quirk" (*née* Victoria Grey).

SHE WEARILY SIGHS—" AND WOMEN MUST WEEP,
AND THE SOONER IT'S OVER THE SOONER TO SLEEP."

## WORLD WEARY.

The radiant firelight softly falls,
With a rosy glow, on the parlor walls:
While a maiden sits with a look of care,
And lists to the wail of the evening air.
There are misty tears in her drooping eyes,
As sorrowful thoughts in her soul arise.
Her heart is heavy, a burning pain
Throbs and thrills through her troubled brain.
She wearily sighs, "and women must weep,
And the sooner it's over the sooner to sleep."

Out on the street, through the frosty air,
The gas-light gleams with a ghostly glare.
Through the wailing wind and the drifting snow,
A homeless woman walks to and fro;
Her heart is heavy, a burning pain
Throbs and thrills through her troubled brain.
No home, no friends and no warm attire,
No easy-chair by a blazing fire.
Women must suffer "and women must weep,
And the sooner it's over the sooner to sleep."

And thus it is ever when trials fall,
Where the firelight glows on the parlor wall;
Or out on the street, where the wild winds blow
And drift and scatter the winter snow,
Like a leafless tree alone and bare,
Is a woman's heart in its wild despair.

When her soul goes forth with a mournful cry,
As the wind with a woeful wail sweeps by.
In wealth or poverty, "Women must weep,
And the sooner it's over the sooner to sleep."

## MIDNIGHT.

The north wind was frigidly blowing,
    With a weary, disconsolate moan.
The stars by black storm clouds were hidden,
    The streets were deserted and lone.
Save the flickering lamps of the city,
    That burned with a dim spectral gleam,
All was wrapped in the mantle of MIDNIGHT
    And darkness was reigning supreme.

Through the dim lonely streets of the city,
    Unmindful of darkness or gale,
There hurried along the damp pavement
    A WOMAN, distracted and pale:
Nor paused she to rest, tho' aweary,
    Nor heeded the rain and the cold,
Till she stood, in the blackness of midnight,
    Where the dark waves of Michigan rolled.

Alone, with her proud spirit broken;
    Alone, with her sorrow and shame;
Alone, with her crushed heart and beauty,
    With neither a home nor a name;
With memories drifting before her,
    That tortured her heart and her brain,
Of friends and companions, once loving,
    That never would love her again.

A dark wave swept onward before her,
    With lofty and foam-laden crest;
Her hair in the north wind was streaming,
    Her thin hands were clasped to her breast.

A plash in the merciless waters,
    A struggle, a gurgle and moan;
The billows rolled wildly above her;
    The desolate pier was alone.

O Death! in thy unknown dominions,
    No pitiless storm-billows roar,
With thee, the worn heart may find refuge,
    Where trouble may haunt it no more.
Thou peace of the sad and the lowly,—
    Thou comfort of all the depressed,
Thy dark mantle hides all our sorrows—
    Thou givest the world-weary rest.

The south wind was tenderly blowing,
    No longer the wild waters rolled,
But gently were dancing and gleaming
    In ripples of purple and gold.
And drifting about on their bosom,
    With glowing clouds floating above,
A pale face stared upward towards HEAVEN,
    Appealing for PITY and LOVE.

## HELEN.*

While her young life was bright and fair
With hope and promise everywhere,
The spoiler came, and at his will
Her beauty paled and passed away,
As fades the splendor of the day
When twilight falls and all is still.

O tranquil slumber! Heavenly birth!
She sleeps to wake no more on earth,
But in a holier atmosphere
Her spirit smiles upon us here,
As peacefully, as from the skies
The stars look down with trembling eyes
Upon the dewy world below,
Whose sorrows she may never know.

Uplifted on the shore of time,
O Death! thy gateway stands sublime.
Beyond there is a brighter shore,
From whence we may return no more.
O unknown boundary that lies
Between the world and Paradise!

* In memory of Helen A. Waters, who died Aug. 11th, 1872.

## TWICE ASLEEP.

A child lies sleeping in calm repose,
As sweet and fair as a dewy rose;

Her little white hands are laid at rest
Over her gently-heaving breast.

Sunny smiles on her red lips play,—
Linger a moment, then pass away.

Forms and faces of earth and air
Flit through her mind while she slumbers there,

Amid the misty and mellow skies,
Their white wings dazzle her dreaming eyes,

Until she wakens in mute dismay,
While her fleeting fancies fade away.

She sleeps again — in her last repose;
She lies like a withered and faded rose.

Over her forehead, pale and fair,
Ripple her tresses of golden hair;

Her little white hands are laid at rest
Over her tranquil and lifeless breast.

Her voice is silent, and, come what may,
No smile will gladden her lips of clay.

For the happy dreams she dreamed are through;
How sweet to hope that they all came true!

## THEN AND NOW.

### THEN.

Long ago sweet Lilian Claire,
    Stood by a window, young and fair;

She smiled to think that her soul was free
    From the earthly cares that were yet to be.

But the smile on her sweet lips died away
    As she thought of her lover, Allen May.

"Ah, me!" she sighed, "if I only knew
    My beautiful day-dreams might come true."

Fond is the love that a woman feels,
    Tender the passion her heart conceals.

She who has truly loved may know
    That love is a woman's heaven below.

These were the thoughts of Lilian Claire
    As she built her castles in the air.

### NOW.

Fifty years have gone away,
    Allen and Lilian are old and gray.

Bright young grandchildren 'round them cling,
    Gay and happy as birds in spring.

Lilian, clasping the old man's hand,
    Proudly looks on the youthful band.

Then softly whispers, sweet and low,
    Just as she used to long ago:

"Allen, our journey is almost through,
    My youthful day-dreams have all come true!"

## SOLOMON RAY.

A HARD, close man was Solomon Ray,
Nothing of value he gave away;
    He hoarded and saved;
    He pinched and shaved;
And the more he had, the more he craved.

The hard-earned dollars he toiled to gain,
Brought him little but care and pain;
    For little he spent,
    And all he lent
He made it bring him twenty per cent.

Such was the life of Solomon Ray;
The years went by, and his hair grew gray,
    His cheeks grew thin,
    And his soul within
Grew hard as the dollars he worked to win.

But he died one day, as all men must,
For life is fleeting and man but dust;
    The heirs were gay
    That laid him away,
And that was the end of Solomon Ray.

They quarreled now, who had little cared
For Solomon Ray while his life was spared;
    His lands were sold,
    And his hard-earned gold
All went to the lawyers, I am told.

Yet men will cheat and pinch and save,
Nor carry their treasures beyond the grave.
　　All their gold some day
　　　Will melt away
Like the selfish savings of Solomon Ray.

## TWO PICTURES.

Two pictures hung on the dingy wall
Of a grand and old Florentine hall;

One of a child, of beauty rare,
With a cherub face and golden hair,

The lovely look of whose radiant eyes
Filled the soul with thoughts of Paradise.

The other face was a visage vile,
Marked with the lines of lust and guile,—

A loathsome being, whose features fell
Brought to the soul weird thoughts of hell.

Side by side, in their frames of gold,
Dingy and dusty, cracked and old,
This is the solemn tale they told:

A youthful painter found one day,
In the streets of Rome, a child at play,

And, moved by the beauty that it bore —
The heavenly look that its features wore —

On a canvas, radiant and grand,
He painted its face with a master hand.

Year after year on his wall it hung,
'Twas ever joyful and always young,—

Driving away all thoughts of gloom,
While the painter toiled in his dingy room.

Like an Angel of Light it met his gaze,
Bringing him dreams of his boyhood days,
Filling his soul with a sense of praise.

His raven ringlets grew thin and gray;
His young ambition all passed away.

Yet he looked for years, in many a place,
To find a contrast to that sweet face.

Through haunts of vice in the night he strayed,
To find some ruin that crime had made.

At last, in a prison cell, he caught
A glimpse of the hideous fiend he sought.

On a canvas weird and wild, but grand,
He painted the face with a master hand.

His task was done; 'twas a work sublime,
An angel of joy and a fiend of crime,—
A lesson of life from the wreck of time.

O crime! with ruin thy road is strown,
The brightest beauty the world has known.

Thy power has wasted, till, in the mind,
No trace of its presence is left behind.

The loathsome wretch in the dungeon low,
With the face of a fiend and a look of woe,

Ruined by revels of crime and sin,
A pitiful wreck of what might have been,

Hated and shunned, and without a home,
Was the *child* that played in the streets of Rome.

## ON THE BANK OF THE MURMURING RILL.

At the foot of a hill by a murmuring rill
        That runs on its way to the sea;
Lived a maiden as fair as a creature of air,
        And as lovely as woman could be.
In the places she strayed, through the beautiful glade
The lovely wild-flowers now blossom and fade,
        Yet lone is the valley to me,
        Lone is the valley to me.

Sweet Marion Glenn, neither language nor pen
        Can picture thy beauty so rare;
What memories rise at the thought of thine eyes
        And thy tresses of ebon black hair!
Thou wilt meet me no more in the low cottage door,
The Summer winds whistle, the Autumn gales roar,
        And the dead leaves are swept through the air,
        The dead leaves are swept through the air.

Yet the clear waters flow, as they did long ago,
        By the cot at the foot of the hill;
And the drooping elms wave o'er a mossy green grave,
        On the bank of the murmuring rill;
While the golden sun gleams, and the silver moon beams
In the day and the night time, on woodlands and streams,
        But the beautiful sleeper is still,
        The beautiful sleeper is still.

ON THE BANK OF THE MURMURING RILL.

## TRUE FRIENDS.

Some souls there are that never change,
 Some friendships that endure;
That neither time nor years estrange,
 Some hearts divine and pure —
And as we meet them here and there
About the world, how dear they are!

And were it not for friends like these,
 To bless our cheerless fate,
The life we live on earth below
 Were more than desolate,
And this dark, lonely world of ours
Were like a garden void of flowers.

## SLEEP.

The summer moon is creeping through the skies,
The evening wind disconsolately sighs;

Hushed are the sounds of toil and busy trade,
The crickets chirp their evening serenade.

The weary laborer slumbers in his cot,
And all his cares of living are forgot:

The children long have ceased their joyous play,
In happy dreams they sleep the night away.

O sleep! thou heavenly balm for human woe,
Thou hidest all our sorrows here below.

In thy embrace, the mourner smiles again,
And aching hearts forget their poignant pain.

While faces marred by lines of worldly care,
Are, by thy touch, made beautiful and fair.

O sleep! thou heavenly balm for human woe,
The common comfort of the proud and low.

## ANOTHER YEAR.

Another year has gone, to come no more;
    Its scenes of joy and hours of grief are done —
'Tis gone where other years have gone before,
    Where all must end that ever was begun;
Where gaunt and gray oblivion loves to dwell,
And infant Time first lisped the hours "farewell."

Below the fleecy folds of drifting snow,
    Like beauty laid at rest, the verdure lies;
Beneath the ice the silent rivers flow,
    The rippling rills are hidden from our eyes.
While time glides by as swiftly as the wind,
And only leaves his memories behind.

The spring-time came, and, ere it passed away,
    The world was robed in beauty everywhere;
The blooming roses and the new-mown hay
    Perfumed the breezes of the summer air;
Then Autumn came, and with her flying gold
The simple story of a year was told.

Farewell, Old Year, for thou art gone at last,
    And Time has borne thee on his hoary wings
Into the silent ages of the past;
    And now another year he proudly brings.
Thy funeral dirge is chanted by the breeze,
Through the bare branches of the leafless trees.

The New Year comes with many frowning fears,
    Yet with a thousand promises of joy;
The sombre shadows of maturer years
    Our youthful fancies and fair dreams destroy:

Yet heavenly Hope looks down with angel eyes
From gleaming, golden gates of Paradise.

Ambition points us to the toilsome way
    That leads to worldly honor and renown;
Yet all life's fleeting phantoms must decay,
    And all our fading laurels totter down,—
While coming bards may sing immortal songs
Of our great failings and stupendous wrongs.

There is one dream that never fades or dies;
    The dream of Heaven. How marvelously grand,
Tho' all life's howling tempests that arise,
    Sweep o'er the rock of ages where we stand;
We glance adown the pathway we have trod,
And leave our imperfections all with God.

O Time! roll down thy ceaseless course of change
    With all thy universal light and shade;
O Mystery! before thy boundless range
    All human understanding falls dismayed;
Thy veil,that puzzles every human brain,
By angels only can be rent in twain.

www.ingramcontent.com/pod-product-compliance
Lightning Source LLC
Chambersburg PA
CBHW020142170426
43199CB00010B/850